DEAD RIKA —

A FOREST LAWN

BY LUKE YANKEE
AND JAMES BONTEMPO

BASED ON THE ONE-ACT PLAY
"SAVE ME A PLACE AT FOREST LAWN"
BY LOREES YERBY

THANK YOU FOR HELPING US ON THIS ★ JOURNEY!

BLESSINGS & LOVE —

Luke & Jim

DRAMATISTS
PLAY SERVICE
INC.

A PLACE AT FOREST LAWN
Copyright © 2007, Luke Yankee and James Bontempo

All Rights Reserved

CAUTION: Professionals and amateurs are hereby warned that performance of A PLACE AT FOREST LAWN is subject to payment of a royalty. It is fully protected under the copyright laws of the United States of America, and of all countries covered by the International Copyright Union (including the Dominion of Canada and the rest of the British Commonwealth), and of all countries covered by the Pan-American Copyright Convention, the Universal Copyright Convention, the Berne Convention, and of all countries with which the United States has reciprocal copyright relations. All rights, including without limitation professional/amateur stage rights, motion picture, recitation, lecturing, public reading, radio broadcasting, television, video or sound recording, all other forms of mechanical, electronic and digital reproduction, transmission and distribution, such as CD, DVD, the Internet, private and file-sharing networks, information storage and retrieval systems, photocopying, and the rights of translation into foreign languages are strictly reserved. Particular emphasis is placed upon the matter of readings, permission for which must be secured from the Authors' agent in writing.

The worldwide English language stock and amateur stage performance rights for A PLACE AT FOREST LAWN are controlled exclusively by DRAMATISTS PLAY SERVICE, INC., 440 Park Avenue South, New York, NY 10016. No professional or nonprofessional performance of the Play may be given without obtaining in advance the written permission of DRAMATISTS PLAY SERVICE, INC., and paying the requisite fee.

Inquiries concerning all other rights should be addressed to International Creative Management, Inc., 825 Eighth Avenue, New York, NY 10019. Attn: Buddy Thomas.

SPECIAL NOTE

Anyone receiving permission to produce A PLACE AT FOREST LAWN is required to give credit to the Authors as sole and exclusive Authors of the Play on the title page of all programs distributed in connection with performances of the Play and in all instances in which the title of the Play appears for purposes of advertising, publicizing or otherwise exploiting the Play and/or a production thereof. The names of the Authors must appear on a separate line, in which no other name appears, immediately beneath the title and in size of type equal to 50% of the size of the largest, most prominent letter used for the title of the Play. No person, firm or entity may receive credit larger or more prominent than that accorded the Authors. The billing must appears as follows:

A PLACE AT FOREST LAWN
by Luke Yankee and James Bontempo

based on the one-act play
"Save Me a Place at Forest Lawn"
by Lorees Yerby

*To our mothers,
Rose Marie Bontempo
and
Eileen Heckart Yankee,
our very own Gertrude and Clara*

ACKNOWLEDGMENTS

A Place at Forest Lawn has been presented in readings and workshop productions in New York City, Los Angeles and Palm Springs, California, with the help of many talented artists, including: Marion Ross, Betty White, Marcia Cross, Barbara Rush, Pat Carroll, Lee Meriwether, Alice Hirson, Gabrielle Carteris, Alan Mandell, Maree Cheatham, Steven Culp, Frank Clem, John McCook, Carol Swarbrick, Karole Foreman, Jason Graae, Millicent Martin, Jim Pirri, Russ Green, Merle Louise, Frances Helm, Jennifer Roszell, Jeff Trachta, Bill Brochtrup, Ian Abercrombie, Jill Andre, Jack Betts, Kerry Anderson, Karis Christensen, David Baecker, Nathan Huntley, Catherine Adkins Suraci, Carol Russo, Elizabeth London, Marilee Warner, Charles Stroud, Mark Ciglar, Carrie Dobro, Diane Ouradnik, John Sgueglia and Don Hill.

Special thanks to Michael Dutton.

NOTES FROM THE PLAYWRIGHTS

A Place at Forest Lawn should not be played for sentimentality but for honesty. The characters are doing the best they can with what they've been given in life. It's about simple truth.

Clara is not mean. She's developed a cantankerous attitude over the years but never intends "hurt" in her dealings with the other characters. She and Jack, though they say awful things to one another, do not do so as "attacks." Their argument at the end of Act One is more like two children fighting without thinking than adults trying to wound each other with calculated cruelty. Clara has a wicked sense of humor that surfaces when it is least expected.

Far from naive, Gertrude has chosen to look at life through rose-colored glasses. She always wants to see the good in people and does her best to please. It's important to remember that, especially in the "Rose Garden/Rosengarten" exchange. The lines about "saying your name the prettier way" are meant to be light and sweet and not in any way derogatory.

As a boss, Jack's a great guy but around his mother, all the old feelings of abandonment and jealousy rise to the top. He blames her for the failures in his life rather than taking responsibility for his actions.

Albert is not a buffoon. Charming and social, he lives in a world of his own creation and believes his stories to be true.

Sonny is the voice of reason and the one person who tells it like it is. He's goodhearted and lives life by his own rules.

Father Gabriel is not a caricature but rather a novice doing what he believes to be right. He goes from unintentionally "playing" at being a priest to becoming one.

The play is to be performed with one intermission on a unit set with different levels representing separate playing areas. Transitions in time and place should be done as simply as possible, mostly through changes in lighting. The car should be suggested by the placement of four stools in a pool of light. The church pews should be suggested by the placement of chairs or simple benches.

A workshop production of A PLACE AT FOREST LAWN was presented at The Promenade Theatre in New York City on October 7, 2002. The stage manager was Christine Catti; the production coordinator was Donald Hill; and the assistant stage manager was Christine Nigro. The cast was as follows:

CLARA OLSEN	Frances Sternhagen
GERTRUDE WYNANT	Marian Seldes
JACK OLSEN	Tony Goldwyn
ALBERT HOGOBARTH	George Grizzard
SONNY	John Glover
FATHER GABRIEL	Anthony Newfield

As winner of the New Noises Festival for drama, A PLACE AT FOREST LAWN received a workshop production at the Perry-Mansfield Performing Arts School (June Lindenmayer and Burgess Clark, Producers) in Steamboat Springs, Colorado on June 21, 2003.

A PLACE AT FOREST LAWN received its world premiere at the Arvada Center for the Arts and Humanities (Kathy Kuehn and Rod Lansberry, Producers) in Arvada, Colorado, on October 18, 2005.

CHARACTERS

CLARA OLSEN — a stern, elderly woman afraid of her own vulnerability.

JACK OLSEN — her son, 40s, a hard-working businessman.

GERTRUDE WYNANT — Clara's best friend for many years, soft and gentle.

ALBERT HOGABARTH — a grand, elderly gentleman from a bygone era.

SONNY —late 30s, a stoned-out, scruffy Harvard graduate who loves life.

FATHER GABRIEL — 20s to 30s, an eager young priest who has recently completed his religious training.

A PLACE AT FOREST LAWN

ACT ONE

As the house lights fade, the strains of a scratchy, old recording of "Blue Moon" plays briefly. Stained-glass lighting represents a church. There is a coffin downstage and a large group of mourners, unseen by the audience. Clara Olsen, an elderly woman, enters and approaches the coffin. She crosses herself and begins to pray but is distracted by the face of the corpse.

CLARA. That mortician should be shot! *(Clara peers at the face and rubs the cheek of the corpse with her gloved finger.)* Max Factor number sixteen. That's a terrible color! He looks like a sun-dried tomato. *(She wipes her finger on a handkerchief, examines the coffin and whistles.)* Nice box! Must be solid mahogany. There goes his daughter's inheritance. *(Clara chuckles to herself as she raps on the side of the coffin. She takes a tape measure out of her purse and checks the width of the coffin.)* Thirty inches — not bad! In the name of the Father and of the Son and of the Holy Ghost. Heavenly Father, if I look that bad in my casket, I ask Your humble permission to come back and get even. Amen. *(An old woman enters. She is Gertrude Wynant, about the same age as Clara. She stands at a distance from the coffin.)* I thought you were right behind me.
GERTRUDE. Better to go now than be interrupted later.
CLARA. Come over here and pay your last respects. *(Gertrude stays where she is, barely looking at the coffin.)*
GERTRUDE. Oh, that's all right, dear. Ever since my Henry died, I don't like to … *(Albert Hogabarth, an ancient but refined-looking older gentleman, enters with a flourish and crosses to the coffin.)*
ALBERT. He looks so peaceful.

CLARA. He should. He's dead.
GERTRUDE. Clara, have some respect for the dearly departed.
ALBERT. He was such a wonderful blackjack player.
GERTRUDE. He was?
CLARA. He was no such thing. He was very religious. I saw him in the front pew every Sunday at Mass. He didn't play cards, didn't smoke and he didn't drink.
GERTRUDE. Good for him.
ALBERT. That was on Sunday. On Saturday he dealt cards like a riverboat gambler, smoked Havana cigars and drank like a sailor on a three-day leave.
CLARA. You're wrong, Albert! You always get things mixed up. I've known him for a very long time and he was dry as dust.
ALBERT. Clara, I knew him much longer than you. We were both contract players at Paramount. He was thrown out of more ladies' dressing rooms than flattened falsies.
CLARA. There's no need to be vulgar. You obviously have him confused with someone else. I did his makeup for every film he was in, all three of them, and he was very respectful.
ALBERT. Clearly, we saw him in a different light. Oh, and he had such a marvelous room. 329. I wonder who gets it?
CLARA. Such a great view.
GERTRUDE. I could make curtains.
ALBERT. I don't care if his name was above the title of *Swampgirls in Love*, he did not deserve that southern exposure. Poor old whoosiz.
CLARA. Don't you remember his name, either?
ALBERT. I always called him "Duke," but he was nothing like the real Duke. That man was one in a million. *(Albert crosses downstage to the coffin with a dramatic flair.)* "And all our yesterdays have lighted fools the way to dusty death."
CLARA. *(Under her breath.)* Ugh, here we go again …
ALBERT. "Out, out, brief candle! Life's but a walking shadow; a poor player, that struts and frets his hour upon the stage, and then is heard no more … " *(Albert exits grandly.)*
CLARA. Enough of this drivel. *(Father Gabriel, a young priest, enters with a white balloon tied to a string.)*
FATHER GABRIEL. As the soul floats heavenward, the gates of our Father's house open welcomingly. "Up, up and away … " *(Father Gabriel releases the balloon and watches it float upward.)*
CLARA. Gabe, do you really think that's necessary?
FATHER GABRIEL. Clara, it's Father Gabriel. Releasing the bal-

loon is supposed to give peace of mind to those left behind. A sort of visual interpretation of the journey to heaven.

CLARA. Seems to me like a waste of a good balloon.

FATHER GABRIEL. It's symbolic.

CLARA. Symbolic of what? It's a wake, not a circus.

FATHER GABRIEL. This is a happy occasion for the soul … to be reunited with the Father in heaven.

CLARA. While the rest of us down here suffer.

FATHER GABRIEL. It is sad for those left behind but we'll all be together again someday.

CLARA. Thanks for the reminder.

FATHER GABRIEL. Clara, that's not what I meant. I'm only trying to say that … uh … we all … uh … I have to go find his family. They asked me to lead them in the Rosary. Have a good day, ladies. *(Father Gabriel exits. Clara looks up at the balloon.)*

CLARA. If he's supposed to guide me back to heaven, I'm in big trouble.

GERTRUDE. He's doing his best, I'm sure.

CLARA. Well, I'm not! I need a priest with guts, not Howdy Doody with a balloon. When we buried Charlie and Henry, those were proper, dignified funerals.

GERTRUDE. Let's not talk about that, dear.

CLARA. Why?

GERTRUDE. I'd just rather not. Let's go, Clara. *(Gertrude turns to Clara and puts her arm in hers and tries to exit.)*

CLARA. Don't you want to say goodbye? I thought you worked in the wardrobe department for that awful Western he was in.

GERTRUDE. That's all right. I didn't really know him that well.

CLARA. C'mon. I've got to mail this letter to Aloysius. Have you got a stamp?

GERTRUDE. Another letter?

CLARA. Futile as it is.

GERTRUDE. Maybe the other ones got lost in the mail to Seattle.

CLARA. Seattle isn't that far away.

GERTRUDE. Well, he works for such a large advertising agency, maybe they lose them. That could be why he never responds.

CLARA. Silence is a response.

GERTRUDE. How can you say that? He never misses your birthday or Christmas.

CLARA. His secretary is most attentive. She's even mastered his signature. *(Gertrude and Clara cross centerstage to the dining room of the*

Hollywood Palms, a run-down retirement hotel. They are shuffling along, clutching cafeteria trays with food. Sounds of noisy patrons resound as they look for a table.) Where shall we sit, Gertrude? I chose yesterday. *(Gertrude surveys the sea of tables.)*
GERTRUDE. Hmmm. Now, let me see ... *(She crosses downstage left.)* Is this one all right?
CLARA. It seems all right ... *(Clara begins to cross to the table but Gertrude stops, looking upward.)*
GERTRUDE. Oh, no. There's a draft there. How about this one?
CLARA. They didn't wipe it yet.
GERTRUDE. We don't have much choice, Clara. *(Clara sees a clean, empty table and walks toward it. She rests her tray on the back of the chair.)*
CLARA. You can have an extra turn tomorrow.
GERTRUDE. *(Whining.)* Now, that wouldn't be fair!
CLARA. Gertrude, the stew is getting cold.
GERTRUDE. All right, but I get an extra turn tomorrow. You'll remember?
CLARA. You may not, but I will. *(Gertrude sets down her lunch and turns to leave.)* Where are you going? *(Looking from side to side, Gertrude whispers to Clara.)*
GERTRUDE. Better to go now than be interrupted later. *(Used to the routine, Clara starts to remove the dishes from the tray and arranges them on the table. She studies Gertrude's tray then looks around to make sure no one is watching. Quickly, Clara switches their desserts. Clara then holds the empty trays at her side. She looks around the room as Gertrude returns to the table.)* Ugh, I hate public toilets.
CLARA. Nothing in life is good that's free, Gertrude. Do you see a cart?
GERTRUDE. No, dear, I don't. Just put them anyplace. *(Clara puts the trays down and sits opposite Gertrude. The ladies simultaneously unfold their napkins with a flourish. They begin to eat. Gertrude stops.)* Oh, that silly new girl. She let the gravy run right into my string beans.
CLARA. I'd take it back if I were you.
GERTRUDE. No, I said to myself after the last time they gave me the wrong thing, I'd never again say a word. Life is too short.
CLARA. But still, the wrong should be corrected. Actually, you'd be doing her a favor.
GERTRUDE. Here ... look! It's not just a drop I'm talking about. There's so much gravy, my string beans ... float! *(Clara leans over*

to Gertrude's plate and looks at the soggy mess in shock.)
CLARA. Oh, it's ridiculous to let them get away with that! Show them. They can see for themselves what they've done wrong.
GERTRUDE. Maybe she said, "Would you like gravy on your string beans?" And maybe I smiled at her while I was nodding my head and talking to you.
CLARA. You shouldn't smile and nod at something you don't want.
GERTRUDE. I was only trying to please. I don't like to talk in the line, anyway. I like to be quiet and look at the food, but you're always trying to tell me something. Half the time I don't know what I've chosen until I have it in my mouth.
CLARA. Let's forget about it, Gertrude. People are watching us. They'll think we're senile. Let's talk about something that will help us digest. Something pleasant.
GERTRUDE. What's pleasant?
CLARA. Why, almost everything except your string beans. It's a beautiful day, don't you think?
GERTRUDE. Well, if you like noise and crowds and squeaking doors … if you like steamy girls slopping your gravy … if you like chipped plates and slippery tables, and …
CLARA. If you persist with your complaints, I'll move to another table, I swear!
GERTRUDE. Well, if you want something pleasant, then let us have silence! *(Forcibly adjusting her napkin, Gertrude stabs her fork into the soggy string beans. Clara takes the envelope from her pocket and looks at it for a long moment, then tears it in half. Both women bend their heads to their food. Light crossfade to a small, isolated area downstage right, which represents the lobby of the Hollywood Palms. Albert eyes all the passers-by from his threadbare "throne" by the door. Jack Olsen, a business executive in his early forties, enters downstage left talking on a cell phone. He carries an overnight bag and a briefcase.)*
JACK. *(Into phone.)* Vanessa, I looked at the proofs for the billboard layout in the cab from the airport. It took me forever to get the hell out of there. The copy doesn't work at all. It needs to be smarter and slicker. Send the new slogans to my Blackberry. And tell the art department to make the color scheme sexier … Yes, I'm sure you know what that means. I've seen you flirt with the UPS guy in the elevator … Yes, I have the bill from the mortuary. I haven't called them yet. I went to the old neighborhood, the house was sold, and everybody I knew was gone. Then, I ran into the

mailman who said that her mail had been forwarded to some rest home. I just walked in … wait a minute, I still have more notes. *(To Albert.)* Excuse me, is this the Hollywood Palms?
ALBERT. Lovely day, isn't it?
JACK. I hadn't noticed. *(To phone.)* Hold on, Vanessa.
ALBERT. Didn't you just come in from that glorious vista?
JACK. *(To phone.)* I said hold on, Vanessa.
ALBERT. Ahh, Vanessa! What a lovely name! I had a lusty scene with Vanessa Redgrave in the film of *Camelot* but it was too steamy for those puritanical censors.
JACK. Is this where Clara Olsen…?
ALBERT. Ah, Clara, a true heartbreaker.
JACK. Clara Olsen?
ALBERT. Oh, yes, yes, a magnificent woman … the sort Robert Mitchum and I used to fight over on the MGM lot. *(Jack looks at something on his Blackberry.)*
JACK. You must be mistaken. *(To phone.)* Whoa, I just got the mock-up for the Michaelson's ad. The coffee can is supposed to be a bright, sunny, "good morning" yellow and the color the art department used is baby shit brown! *(Albert gives him a distasteful look.)* Don't blame the digital picture, I know what baby shit looks like and this is it … no, I haven't changed a diaper lately, smart-ass, but it's still the wrong color. Go talk to them … now, please, and call me when it's done. *(He ends the call and turns to Albert.)* Now, what can you tell me about Clara?
ALBERT. My Clara, a vixen! Never gave me a second glance. I used to tease her when she was doing my makeup at RKO that I wouldn't wait forever but, honestly young man, I would have.
JACK. I'm sorry, sir …
ALBERT. Call me Albert. Everyone does.
JACK. Is that your name?
ALBERT. Why would they call me something other than my name?
JACK. I need some information. *(Something in Jack's coat pocket beeps. He takes out his phone and reads a text message.)* Damn them! *(He talks as he busily types a text message.)* What part of "sexy" don't you understand? Get it right. *(He sends the message.)*
ALBERT. My, you do have a lot of toys.
JACK. Just for my work. Do you remember Clara?
ALBERT. Remember her? Young man, both my mind and memory are strong, unlike that old sot Richard Burton. He could never

remember who he was with, much less how old she was.
JACK. I need you to tell me what you know about her.
ALBERT. A gentleman never reveals a lady's charms.
JACK. We're talking about my mother. *(Albert sits up abruptly.)*
ALBERT. I see. If you want to know anything about dear Clara, you should ask the genteel and elegant Gertrude Wynant.
JACK. Aunt Gertrude? *(Albert's face clouds with a puzzled look.)* We're not related, but that's what I always called her. *(Nodding his head, Albert deftly slips an antique pocket watch from his vest and studies it lovingly.)*
ALBERT. It's time for the evening repast. Go downstairs to the dining room and look for a ceiling fan. Then find the table farthest away from it and that's where your quest will end.
JACK. Thank you, sir. *(His cell phone rings again. To phone:)* What is it now, Vanessa?
ALBERT. Slow down, young man. Enjoy the day, for it's too quickly gone, never to return. I said that once to a contract player on the lot at Columbia. She stayed in my bungalow for three glorious days. We lived on soda crackers and creme brulée. *(Jack nods as he exits. Crossfade to Clara and Gertrude in the dining room, who have been eating in silence. As Clara shovels spoonfuls of custard into her mouth, Gertrude looks up at her. After a long moment, Gertrude breaks the silence.)*
GERTRUDE. I never did like custard. My Henry loved it. So, now I eat it because it makes me feel closer to him.
CLARA. Probably better for you than Henry was. *(Gertrude looks at Clara in shock.)*
GERTRUDE. Oh, Clara! *(Jack enters downstage on his phone. Clara's back is to him.)*
JACK. *(To phone.)* Tell Charlie I'll make it up to him … yes, "again" and don't give me that, I'm doing the best I can. That's right, if the judge had awarded you sole custody, we wouldn't be having this conversation, but she didn't … No, Linda, it can't be helped. My mother died … no, I don't know when it happened … well, she didn't like you, either. *(Jack ends the call.)* Aunt Gertrude! How wonderful to see you! *(Clara turns around to face Jack.)*
CLARA. Well, look what the cat dragged in! *(Jack approaches the table in a state of disbelief. Clara turns around and stares at him.)*
JACK. Holy shit! You're supposed to be dead!
CLARA. It's good to see you, too.
JACK. You think this is funny?

CLARA. Nothing to do with you has ever been funny.
JACK. That makes two of us!
CLARA. Keep your voice down. This is where I live.
JACK. You live here?
CLARA. Yes, and I won't have you embarrassing me.
JACK. Embarrassing you? How do you think I feel? Your phone's been cut off, you seem to vanish off the face of the earth, and then, out of the blue, I get an outrageous bill for a mausoleum.
CLARA. Was it pink Italian marble?
JACK. I don't know! All I saw was the price.
CLARA. I hope they got it right.
JACK. I thought you were dead!
CLARA. So, you scampered down here to bury me but since you can't you're in a snit.
JACK. I left my job in the middle of a new campaign that's practically killing me and broke my ass to get down here and deal with this today. I had to go by the old house to find out you sold it over a year ago. I even called the police. If it hadn't been for some tired, old windbag upstairs who claims you're a "vixen," I wouldn't have known where to find you.
CLARA. If you came to pay your respects, then be respectful. *(She grandly turns to Gertrude.)* Gertrude, you remember my son, Aloysius.
JACK. My name is Jack. You know that. It's been Jack since I was sixteen. Please don't pretend you don't remember that.
CLARA. What I remember, Aloysius, is that I gave you that name to honor my father's father.
JACK. Didn't everyone call Great-Grandfather Aloysius "Bud"?
CLARA. I certainly didn't.
GERTRUDE. Bud sounds like such a friendly name.
JACK. I've missed you, Aunt Gertrude. *(Jack kisses Gertrude on the cheek. She embraces him warmly.)*
GERTRUDE. I'm so glad to see you. Oh, Ally, you've gotten so tall!
JACK. You've been saying that since I was in the third grade. And please, call me Jack.
GERTRUDE. Certainly, "Jack." Clara, isn't this a nice surprise?
CLARA. I hate surprises. Finish your custard. Here comes Sonny. *(Clara rises and crosses downstage followed by Gertrude and Jack.)* There's my boy! Right on time, too! *(Sonny, the scruffy-looking driver, enters reading a tattered copy of Kafka's* Metamorphosis *with a joint tucked behind his ear. Music blares through his iPod.)*
GERTRUDE. Sonny, you need a haircut.

CLARA. Or a hairnet. *(Slipping off the headset, Sonny takes another drag.)*
SONNY. How was the custard? Isn't Monday custard day?
CLARA. What a memory! Sonny, this is my son, Alo ... I mean Jack.
SONNY. Your son, huh? *(Sonny wipes his hand on the seat of his pants and offers it to Jack.)*
JACK. How do you do?
SONNY. Hey, man, good to meet ya.
GERTRUDE. Jack, this is Mr. Schlomo Rose Garden.
JACK. Schlomo?
SONNY. Just call me "Sonny."
JACK. Rose Garden?
SONNY. It's actually "Rosengarten."
GERTRUDE. *(Whispering, smiles politely.)* I know, dear, but just because you were born into the Jewish faith doesn't mean you can't say your name the prettier way. Everyone likes rose gardens. That's why they have one at the White House.
JACK. "Schlomo Rosengarten"? I thought I had it bad with Johann Aloysius Lars Olsen.
SONNY. You did. Your initials spell "Ja Lo" but you don't have nearly as nice a booty. Ladies, your chariot awaits. *(Sonny takes a joint from behind his ear and lights up. He and the ladies cross downstage to four stools representing a car. Jack follows.)*
CLARA. Sonny's taking us to the market. Aloysius, you can carry the bags.
GERTRUDE. My geraniums told me that spring is just around the corner.
CLARA. Your geraniums told you?
GERTRUDE. Yes, dear. I sing to them every day and they talk to me.
SONNY. Same thing happens to me, Gertrude. My plants like talkin' to me too. *(He takes a toke on the joint. Gertrude presents him with something wrapped in a white paper napkin.)*
GERTRUDE. It's your favorite.
SONNY. An onion roll! No way! *(Clara and Gertrude exit. Sonny turns to Jack.)* Nice suit. Armani?
JACK. Versace.
SONNY. Whatever. *(Lighting suggests a modest living room/kitchen area. Clara enters her apartment and takes off her coat. She crosses to the sofa and picks up an oversized man's cardigan sweater with the letters HW monogrammed over the heart and gently puts it on. She cross-*

es to the mirror.)
CLARA. That's better. *(Clara begins to sing the melody of "Blue Moon.")* "Blue Moon … da da da da da alone, da da da da da my heart, da da da love of my own … " *(She pulls the sweater a little tighter around her, continuing to sing.)* You'd know the words. You always did. *(She sighs deeply and looks upward.)* Okay, he's here now. Thanks for that, but I'm not sure what to do next. I didn't expect him to be so hard. I don't remember that about him. *(She pulls the sweater a little tighter around herself. She grabs her side in pain.)* My darling, when you get a second, would you throw a few extra prayers my way? I think I'm going to need all the help I can get. *(Jack enters with a bag of groceries.)*
JACK. That guy drives like a maniac.
CLARA. He's so high most of the time, he doesn't notice.
JACK. Wonderful. You put your safety in the hands of that low-life druggie.
CLARA. He's a Harvard graduate.
JACK. Okay, I don't want to argue.
CLARA. Speaking of arguing, how is that ex-wife of yours?
JACK. You mean Linda?
CLARA. Oh, is there more than one? *(Jack rubs his face with his hand. Clara notices the ring on his finger.)* I see you're wearing your father's Army ring. I wondered where it went. *(Jack looks at the ring and then back to her.)*
JACK. Dad wanted me to have it.
CLARA. He wanted you to have everything.
JACK. This is all I took.
CLARA. No, it's not.
JACK. What does that mean?
CLARA. Never mind, "Aloysius."
JACK. Okay, so why did you have the Forest Lawn bill sent to me?
CLARA. I thought you might want to help out an old lady.
JACK. Where's the money from the house?
CLARA. It didn't sell for all that much, and once your father's pension ran out I needed something to live on. This place isn't cheap. It was in all those letters I sent you.
JACK. What's your point?
CLARA. You never come to visit, you don't answer my letters and I've never even met my grandson. The only time you show any interest in me is when you think I'm dead.
JACK. Okay, score one for Clara. Can we talk about this Italian mar-

ble mausoleum for seventy-five grand? *(Clara heads for the bedroom.)*
CLARA. Not now we can't.
JACK. Where you going?
CLARA. To get ready for bed. *(Without turning around, Clara points to a closet.)* All my papers are in the shoebox in the closet.
JACK. Wait a minute ... *(Clara exits. Jack crosses to the closet and looks through the clothing. Unseen by Jack, Sonny enters carrying Jack's briefcase.)*
SONNY. Don't think her clothes will fit you. *(Jack whirls around, startled.)*
JACK. What the hell do you want?
SONNY. You left your briefcase in the car.
JACK. Fine. Thank you. Goodbye.
SONNY. You are way too tense, man. Chill out. *(Sonny crosses and sits downstage, followed by Jack.)*
JACK. Don't you have to drive somebody somewhere?
SONNY. Always. But that's one of the perks of being my own boss. I can't fire me.
JACK. You can go, "Schlomo." Your services aren't needed here. *(Sonny rises and starts for the door.)*
SONNY. Don't turn chicken and run.
JACK. Where do you get off calling me a chicken?
SONNY. Look, man, I just call 'em like I see 'em.
JACK. You don't know the first thing about me.
SONNY. I know you got no balls.
JACK. You brain-dead loser ...
SONNY. Hey, cut the flattery and wake up. That old lady needed you and somehow she managed to get you here. Don't waste any more time. *(Sonny scratches his beard and exits. Jack takes a shoebox out of the closet. He removes an old "blue ribbon" award hanging on a looped piece of string and looks at it for a long time. Jack puts the ribbon around his neck. He reaches for another box.)*
JACK. "Wedding shoes." *(He lifts out a dainty white peau de soie slipper and discovers a stack of letters neatly tied with a lavender silk ribbon. He looks toward the closed bedroom door. Taking one of the letters, Jack carefully opens it.)* "My dear one, I've never been very good with words, but that's no surprise to you. Yet, whenever I take your hand, you know what's in my heart." *(Clara quietly enters and recites the rest of the letter from memory.)*
CLARA and JACK. " ... from the moment we met, I knew we'd be together ... "

CLARA. " ... today, tomorrow and always. My soul is yours." *(After a moment, she quietly takes the letter from him and gathers the rest.)* I loved him with all my heart. *(She turns and starts back to her bedroom.)* And he'd want me to have the Italian marble.
JACK. I never knew how much you loved him.
CLARA. Of course not. People didn't talk about that sort of thing. Besides, it was none of your business. *(Beat.)* You were always such a busy little boy. Hardly ever home once your father got you that secondhand bike.
JACK. It was new to me. I loved that bike.
CLARA. The only way I could ever get you to do something you didn't want to was to tell you that you couldn't ride it for a week.
JACK. But you never took it away.
CLARA. Didn't have to. Most of the time. You were a good boy. *(Softly, he begins to sing the melody of "Little Brown Jug.")*
JACK. "Ha, ha, ha, you and me, little brown jug, don't I love thee!"
CLARA. Your father and I couldn't believe you drank that whole quart of beer.
JACK. I was the only first-grader with a hangover. *(Clara looks at the crumpled award hanging around his neck.)*
CLARA. I thought I threw that ribbon out.
JACK. You told me when we won this at the swing dance contest that you'd keep it forever. *(Jack gets up from the floor and awkwardly jitterbugs as he sings the song again. His volume and the dance both grow in intensity.)* "Ha, ha, ha, you and me. Little brown jug, don't I love thee!" Remember the day you taught me how to jitterbug to that song? You said it was the best way to remember the evils of drinking.
CLARA. Which you seemed to forget once you got into high school.
JACK. Let's dance. *(The dance continues.)*
CLARA. Thank God you got my sense of music. Your father had no rhythm. *(Jack takes off the ribbon and, unseen by Clara, slides it into his shirt pocket.)*
JACK. Maybe I'll stay a day or two.
CLARA. Why would you want to do that?
JACK. I guess I missed you.
CLARA. Really? Well, that's nice.
JACK. Yeah ... and besides, I should get your bills straightened out.
CLARA. They're not in disarray, they just need to be paid. *(Jack's cell phone rings.)* Your slaves must need you. *(Jack looks at the cell phone.)*
JACK. Yeah, Vanessa, what is it now? ... Okay, I've got a few min-

utes, run them by me ... *(Clara watches for a moment then crosses downstage to the dining room area, joining Gertrude at the table as the lights crossfade. The ladies finish their lunch and sip tea.)*
GERTRUDE. It's sweet that after all the time he's been away, he wants to be close to you now.
CLARA. He's in the same room but never gets off that damn cell phone. He's as absent as his father was. *(Gertrude looks up and sees Albert holding a tray.)*
GERTRUDE. Clara, don't look now, but Albert Hogabarth is in the line. *(She waves furiously to him.)*
CLARA. He made such a spectacle of himself at what's-his-name's wake.
GERTRUDE. Edgar. His name was Edgar.
CLARA. You said you didn't know him very well.
GERTRUDE. But I remember his name. It's the least we can do for him.
CLARA. Ugh! You'd think Albert would have more sense at his age. *(Clara fixes her hair. Gertrude motions Albert towards them. He steps out of line and shuffles to the table.)*
GERTRUDE. Now, Clara, be charitable. He's lonely. He just wants your company.
CLARA. No man just wants your company. I remember him from when I worked on the lot. That man tried to date every girl in the makeup department. But some weren't as smart as I was.
ALBERT. As I live and breathe!
CLARA. *(Mumbles under her breath.)* Barely.
ALBERT. Gertrude, how lovely to see you again. *(He kisses Gertrude's hand.)*
GERTRUDE. Hello, Albert.
ALBERT. And Clara! My dear, you're looking particularly radiant today.
CLARA. Must be gas.
ALBERT. Clara, would you do me the honor of allowing me to escort you to the concert in Plummer Park this evening? It's Mozart in the open air and I don't mind telling you that I had to pull in a few favors from an old chum to secure the tickets.
CLARA. Albert, you and I both know that concert is free. No, thank you, I have other plans. I'm untangling my phone cord.
ALBERT. Ah, *quel domage. (He turns to Gertrude as though she's just arrived.)* Gertrude, could I interest you in accompanying me to the concert? *The Magic Flute* under the stars? What do you say? *(Before*

Gertrude can answer, Clara jumps in.)
CLARA. Oh no you don't! You don't play second fiddle to anyone.
GERTRUDE. Thank you, Albert. Maybe another time. We could pull up another chair if you'd like …
CLARA. We were just leaving!
ALBERT. More's the pity to deprive this humble establishment of such grace and elegance. You know, when I was Kirk Douglas' stand-in on *Spartacus* …
CLARA. You'd better hurry or you'll miss the tapioca.
ALBERT. Ah, quite so. Sadly, I take my leave, fair maidens, as I proceed to the flan, the creme brulée, the mousse au … *(Clara squeezes her lemon into her tea with great force.)*
CLARA. It's tapioca!
ALBERT. Clara, if you wish it so, then it shall be. "A rose by any other name … " So ladies, my blushing damsels at the banquet, may I say, *au revoir? (Gertrude giggles.)*
GERTRUDE. *Au revoir!*
CLARA. *A bien toot! (Heading back toward the line, Albert sees an orange left on a table. He makes a beeline for it and quickly stuffs it into his pocket.)*
GERTRUDE. You could be a little nicer to him, Clara.
CLARA. I made the mistake of sitting next to him once at a travelogue. And just as we were flying over the Andes, he reached right over in my lap and took my hand in his! Oh, the mush of it all! *(Unseen by Clara, Gertrude takes the hand Albert kissed and gently brushes it against her cheek. Clara notices Father Gabriel walking toward their table.)* Looks like things are going from bad to worse.
FATHER GABRIEL. Hello, ladies. How is your day?
CLARA. What is it now, Gabe?
FATHER GABRIEL. As the new curate of the Senior Citizen's Affirmative Action Association, I'm soliciting volunteers for the "Lend a Smile" program at the Angels of Mercy Hospital.
GERTRUDE. What is that, exactly?
FATHER GABRIEL. All sorts of things but mostly just helping people feel better.
GERTRUDE. I could do that.
FATHER GABRIEL. Excellent. Can you start this afternoon?
GERTRUDE. I think so.
CLARA. Father Walsh never did anything like that.
FATHER GABRIEL. Well, I'm not Father Walsh.
CLARA. You got that right. Aren't you supposed to be helping the

senior citizens? Isn't that why you were sent here, Gabe?
FATHER GABRIEL. I am. Getting you involved as volunteers will give you a new lease on life.
CLARA. Thanks, but I'm not quite done with this one yet. Why do you have to stir things up for no good reason?
FATHER GABRIEL. Like it or not, we have to embrace change.
CLARA. I don't have any problem with change when it makes sense, but letting a balloon go during a wake is just plain silly.
FATHER GABRIEL. It's symbolic.
CLARA. And I'm not the "lend a smile" type.
FATHER GABRIEL. It's never too late to change, Clara.
CLARA. If you want to make a change, then let women be priests. When's that going to happen, Gabe?
FATHER GABRIEL. Clara, please, it's FATHER Gabriel. I don't understand why you won't address me with my proper title of respect.
CLARA. When you've earned it, you'll get it.
FATHER GABRIEL. You mean when you get things your way.
CLARA. No, I mean when you've earned it. Now beat it, Gabe. *(Gladly accepting the dismissal, Father Gabriel exits.)* I hope he's sick the day they bury me.
GERTRUDE. Clara, you know I don't like it when you talk like that.
CLARA. Why? It's the truth.
GERTRUDE. It's not time for you to go yet.
CLARA. I'll go when it's time and I hope it's sooner rather than later. I'll be very happy when I'm dead. *(Gertrude slams her fork down.)*
GERTRUDE. Now you've done it.
CLARA. Done what?
GERTRUDE. I'm so upset, I can't eat another bite!
CLARA. *(In a hushed whisper.)* What have I said? Surely at our age we can talk about dying.
GERTRUDE. My doctor said I could live to be one hundred if I wanted.
CLARA. I'm sure you will, Gertrude. You'll outlast all of us.
GERTRUDE. *(Almost yelling in fear.)* OH GOD! I DON'T WANT TO BE THE LAST ONE!
CLARA. SHHHH! Do you want everyone to hear you?
GERTRUDE. I don't care!
CLARA. What would God think of talk like that? He'll take you when He's good and ready.
GERTRUDE. I hope He doesn't just forget about me and let me

go on and on.

CLARA. He wouldn't do that. He's responsible for getting us here and responsible for getting us back.

GERTRUDE. I'd hate to think it had all been a donkey race.

CLARA. Donkeys are too stubborn to race, Gertrude.

GERTRUDE. What kind of race do I mean then? A greyhound race. You know, where they keep the wooden rabbit just ahead of the dogs … and then at the finish line, they just take it away.

CLARA. Who?

GERTRUDE. Oh, Clara, I saw a greyhound race once … it was just terrible … those poor things … they didn't know where it went.

CLARA. Bosh, dogs love to run.

GERTRUDE. No, they don't. And now I've reached the end of the race and I can't find the wooden rabbit … *(Her face begins to crumble.)*

CLARA. Oh, Gertrude! Forget I ever mentioned it! *(Gertrude's eyes are filled with tears.)*

GERTRUDE. Forgive me, Clara. I didn't think I'd still be so frightened. I thought I'd be ready by now. I thought I'd have all my letters burned and a new dress with big seams and a manicure … but I'm not old enough … and I'm not tired enough … and I'm not sick enough! *(Deeply moved, Clara takes Gertrude's hand in hers.)*

CLARA. Oh, my dear, sweet friend. Everyone is terrified. Really. We're all like children about things that go bump in the night. But somehow we overcome most of our fears. At least enough to keep moving. *(Gertrude dries her eyes.)*

GERTRUDE. Well, that's what I want, Clara. I just want to keep moving forward. I can't go until all the "t's" are crossed and "i's" are dotted.

CLARA. Good girl! Let's keep our heads up and our chests out.

GERTRUDE. I don't think I'm quite up to marching.

CLARA. I know, dear, but ignoring things never makes them go away.

GERTRUDE. You're right, Clara. I'm sure you're right. *(Beat.)* Have you made your plans?

CLARA. Of course I have. *(She raises her teacup and speaks grandly.)* I've arranged for a place at Forest Lawn.

GERTRUDE. Oh, you make it sound so glamorous!

CLARA. What's good enough for Jean Harlow is good enough for Clara Olsen. Have you made your plans?

GERTRUDE. Well, I thought I'd like to be cremated.

CLARA. Don't be so old-fashioned.
GERTRUDE. Who's old-fashioned? I'm thinking of space.
CLARA. Why do you want to be burned up? Who do you think you are, Joan of Arc?
GERTRUDE. Oh, Clara!
CLARA. You can end up in a plastic urn next to somebody's bowling trophy tied with a balloon to carry you back to Jesus! But me, I'm going to have my own pink Italian marble mausoleum. I am damned if I'm going leave this world in the same shoddy way I entered! *(Lights crossfade to another playing area representing a hospital office. Father Gabriel makes notes on his clipboard. He stops and begins mimicking Clara.)*
FATHER GABRIEL. "Aren't you supposed to be helping the senior citizens? Isn't that why you were sent here, Gabe? Father Walsh never did anything like that, Gabe. I'm not the 'lend a smile' type, Gabe. Let women be priests, Gabe. When's that going to happen, Gabe? Gabe. Gabe. Gabe!" *(Gertrude enters, laughing.)*
GERTRUDE. Oh, you sound just like Clara! *(Father Gabriel turns abruptly.)*
FATHER GABRIEL. Mrs. Wynant. I'm so glad you came.
GERTRUDE. Please, call me Gertrude.
FATHER GABRIEL. Of course. The hospital is in desperate need of more volunteers.
GERTRUDE. I could bake some chocolate chip cookies.
FATHER GABRIEL. That's a lovely thought, Gertrude, but I'm sure the hospital dietician would have a few things to say about that.
GERTRUDE. What harm could it do? It's my secret recipe. Clara loves them.
FATHER GABRIEL. I'll bet they're delicious, but that may have to wait.
GERTRUDE. Certainly, I want to help. Just tell me what you need.
FATHER GABRIEL. For now, it would be a great help if you could alphabetize these files. *(Father Gabriel pulls out the chair so Gertrude can sit at the desk.)*
GERTRUDE. Goodness, there sure are a lot of them.
FATHER GABRIEL. Just do what you can. *(Beat.)* I know it doesn't seem all that exciting, but every little bit helps. Remember the mustard seed. *(Gertrude stares at him blankly.)* From a tiny seed a massive tree grew.
GERTRUDE. Oh, I understand.

FATHER GABRIEL. Wonderful! But first, let me give you the ground rules. You must sign in and out for each shift, clothes always neat and clean, no perfume is allowed in case someone is allergic … *(Gertrude looks truly overwhelmed.)* I'll give you a printed list.
GERTRUDE. That would be a big help.
FATHER GABRIEL. Good. Now, you see that door? *(Gertrude leans toward his point, nodding.)*
GERTRUDE. Isn't that the nursery? I pressed my nose up against the window and cooed at them for a while on the way in. Oooh, I love babies.
FATHER GABRIEL. That's the baby holding room. Those infants are high-risk babies of alcoholics and drug users. It's tragic, but they are most likely all going to die.
GERTRUDE. You can't mean that. They're so tiny and precious.
FATHER GABRIEL. That's why the hospital instituted the baby holding program. They need to know that someone in this life cares about them.
GERTRUDE. Oh, can I do that? I love holding babies.
FATHER GABRIEL. It's a highly specialized program with a rigorous training regimen.
GERTRUDE. Just to hold a baby?
FATHER GABRIEL. Gertrude, you cannot go in there. Those babies are fragile and any unnecessary stimuli could be fatal for them. For now, just take care of the files. I have to go upstairs and serve Holy Communion to a few patients. I'll check on you later. *(Father Gabriel exits. Gertrude looks at the mound of files and then shuffles a few halfheartedly. After a moment she rises and crosses to the nursery area. She slips on a sterile paper gown and gloves and then walks into an area with several bassinets and slowly crosses to them. Her eyes fill with joy. She picks up a tiny bundle and pulls back the pink blanket to see a tiny baby, shivering.)*
GERTRUDE. Hello, little one. My name is Gertrude. I am so glad to have found you. What's your name, precious? *(Gertrude looks at the miniscule wrist tag.)* Mai Ling … what a pretty name. Mai Ling, I'm here for you. Don't worry. Don't be scared. I love you. *(Gertrude sits.)* What a pretty little girl you are. When you grow up, I'll teach you how to roller skate. Don't laugh. *(Alone in the room, Gertrude smiles lovingly at Mai Ling, asleep in her arms.)* I used to roller skate every Saturday and I was good. I made my own costume … a red skirt with a white blouse and a blue bolero jacket and I always wore ribbons in my hair. *(She looks down at the

baby.) I guess you kids today would say I looked slammin'. *(Leaning back, Gertrude continues to rock.)* That's where I met him. He was such a skinny boy ... and so shy. He skated up to me and tried to speak so many times that day. Finally, he stammered, "Hello, my name is Henry Wynant," and then he crashed into the wall. I said I would go to the dance with him. He came to my house to pick me up and I insisted he meet my parents, which they don't do nowadays. He called my dad "sir" and my mother "ma'am" and he gave me the most beautiful corsage. It was white gardenias. I can still smell them when I close my eyes. The aroma was so thick and lush you could float on it ... and I did. That night I decided Henry Wynant was the man I would one day marry. We were together for forty-eight years. I held his hand, like I'm holding yours, the night he died. He was very weak from the cancer by then and could barely speak, but his eyes ... his eyes were as vibrant as that day at the roller rink. Henry began to whisper something to me but I couldn't hear him so I leaned my head close to his lips. He kissed me on the cheek and in a raspy voice, he said goodbye. A moment later, he left me ... for the last time. *(Gertrude looks at the quivering infant. Her eyes fill with sadness.)* Don't you leave me too. *(Crossfade to Jack sitting at the elaborately set table with neatly stacked piles of bills and documents. He talks on his cell phone.)*

JACK. *(Into phone.)* ... But they all say "lab tests" ... I'm not questioning your skills, but I need to know what kind of tests my mother has been having ... hold on, please. *(He presses his call waiting button.)* Jack Olsen ... Vanessa, this is not a good time ... tell him you couldn't reach me. *(He presses the call button again.)* Okay, what's her doctor's number? ... *(He scribbles on an envelope. Remembering something, he pockets the cell phone and bolts to the toaster oven and removes a pan of burnt rolls.)* Shit! *(He tries in vain to scrape the blackened rolls, burning his hand in the process.)* Shit, shit, shit! *(Clara enters from outside to all the banging and clattering. Jack turns and sees her, forcing a warm smile.)*

CLARA. What's that smell?

JACK. Hi! Dinner is almost ready!

CLARA. What? *(Jack points to the elaborately set table.)*

JACK. Since you didn't go with Aunt Gertrude to volunteer at the hospital this afternoon ...

CLARA. I don't like hospitals. And I don't like volunteering. How did you know about that?

JACK. I ran into Sonny.

CLARA. I wish he'd learn to keep his mouth shut when he's high.
JACK. Anyway, I thought I'd fix your dinner so you wouldn't have to eat alone. Give you a break from that dingy dining room.
CLARA. I like the dining room. All my friends are there.
JACK. I thought a change of pace might do you some good. *(Clara makes her way to the table and sits.)*
CLARA. What are we having? *(Jack pulls dishes out of the fridge.)*
JACK. For Madame today we will start with a Waldorf salad.
CLARA. Is that the kind with apples and nuts?
JACK. That's right.
CLARA. I can't eat nuts anymore. Diverticulitis.
JACK. Well, you can pick the nuts out. *(Clara pokes at her salad.)*
CLARA. My, so many nuts! *(Picking out the nuts, Clara places them on the table.)*
JACK. The next course will be Quiche Alsace Lorraine.
CLARA. Quiche Lorraine has no personality.
JACK. What?
CLARA. I had that once before and it was bland.
JACK. I thought you weren't supposed to have spicy foods. *(Clara plays with the nuts she's placed on the table.)*
CLARA. I'm not supposed to, but nobody ever croaked from a little Tabasco sauce. Any mashed potatoes? I love mashed potatoes.
JACK. NO! I did not fix mashed potatoes, I browned some Parker House rolls.
CLARA. Smells like you blackened them. May one hope for some dessert?
JACK. I bought a chocolate cake from Tortelli's Bakery.
CLARA. Now you're talkin'! *(Jack thrusts the cake onto the table in front of Clara with a thud.)*
JACK. Eat the cake! Harden your arteries! Have a field day! *(Clara looks shocked at his outburst.)* I was trying to do something nice for you!
CLARA. Yes, I can see that.
JACK. Sorry. My mistake. I guess nothing ever changes. *(Jack takes the untouched plates of food and dumps them into the sink. He picks up the shoebox filled with bills.)* Now, about these bills. *(Clara digs into her piece of cake.)*
CLARA. Thanks for paying them.
JACK. I didn't say I was paying them. I want to know what they're for.
CLARA. You can read, can't you?

JACK. That doesn't tell me what they're for. The doctor bills I can figure out, but why so many lab tests?
CLARA. At my age, they test you for everything.
JACK. Are you sick? *(Clara waves him off.)* And why do you need a mausoleum? There's a spot waiting for you next to Dad.
CLARA. You can have that, too. I'm striking out on my own.
JACK. And you want me to pay for it?
CLARA. Think of it as a payback for raising you so well.
JACK. You're not serious?!
CLARA. I'm cold. Hand me my sweater. *(Shaking his head, Jack crosses to the chair and picks up the sweater, staring at it.)*
JACK. This isn't Dad's.
CLARA. Nope. *(Looking more closely at the sweater, Jack examines the monogram.)*
JACK. HW. Is this…?
CLARA. That belonged to the man who wrote me those letters.
JACK. Henry Wynant? Aunt Gertrude's husband?
CLARA. Your father was a very nice man but I didn't love him. *(Beat.)* Don't look at me like that. He didn't love me either.
JACK. What an ass I've been. I was beginning to think I'd misjudged you, but I was right all along.
CLARA. Right about what?
JACK. When I walked in and saw you two together.
CLARA. You saw nothing.
JACK. You were in his arms!
CLARA. He was comforting me, that's all. Stop jumping to conclusions.
JACK. Cut the crap. If I hadn't walked in, you'd have been rolling around on the floor like a couple of dogs in heat.
CLARA. You're disgusting.
JACK. And you're hilarious.
CLARA. God, help me.
JACK. You pick the strangest times to get religious.
CLARA. All I have left is my faith.
JACK. You're in good company. Mary Magdalene was a whore too.
CLARA. Self-righteous, just like your father. Henry was there for me. I needed someone to help me.
JACK. Help you what?
CLARA. Never mind.
JACK. No, you started this. Help you what?! Steal your best friend's husband? Find new ways to cheat on the man you married, who

loved you and gave you a home? Tell me, "Mother," you needed someone to help you do what?!
CLARA. To help me get through the grief of hating my own son.
(A long, painful silence before Jack finally speaks.)
JACK. Wow. Nice to finally know the truth.
CLARA. That's not it. Not all of it, anyway. When your father and I got married all he ever talked about was having a son. I was young and eager to be a good wife so when you were born, I felt like I'd made us a family. But soon, I realized all he cared about was you. I'd done my service for the cause. He had his son and for all he gave a damn, I was invisible.
JACK. I don't believe Dad was like that.
CLARA. Of course you don't. He was a saint to you.
JACK. Leave him alone. He didn't cheat on you.
CLARA. Yes, I'm afraid he did.
JACK. Liar!
CLARA. He cheated on me with you.
JACK. Don't try to pin this on me.
CLARA. I'm tired now, Jack. Please, leave.
JACK. Not a problem.
CLARA. I don't want Gertrude to know. She can never know.
JACK. Don't worry, I don't hurt the people I love. Oh, and you can forget about the mausoleum. It's not going to happen. *(Jack leaves in silence. Clara wraps the sweater tightly around herself and stares after her son. She begins to cry.)*

End of Act One

ACT TWO

Lights up. Immediately following, Jack crosses downstage and bumps into Albert.

ALBERT. What's your rush, young man?
JACK. None of your goddamn business.
ALBERT. Ah, it must be a woman ... intoxicating creatures.
JACK. What is it with all you people sticking your noses where they don't belong?
ALBERT. Did I ever tell you that as a young man I once played a love scene with Olivia de Havilland? *(Jack stops in his tracks.)*
JACK. Look, Albert, this isn't the right time for a story.
ALBERT. Story? More than a story. An epic.
JACK. Not now, please.
ALBERT. Young man, there are three things in life that cannot be taken for granted: women, liquor and gambling. No matter how you may wish it otherwise, the world would be a desolate place without them.
JACK. Albert, you're only making things worse.
ALBERT. What could she have done that was so completely beyond reproach?
JACK. What are you talking about?
ALBERT. Your mother used to go on about you constantly, but that has waned in recent months to an occasional lament. *Finita la comedia.* The well is dry.
JACK. If you're going to talk about Clara, I've got to have a lot to drink.
ALBERT. Many's the problem I've tried to wash away with liquor only to have it return with the morning tide.
JACK. You have no idea.
ALBERT. Sadly, I do, but it's cleverly masked beneath this charming facade.
JACK. So, you're hiding too?
ALBERT. All the world's a stage. *(Jack starts to exit. Albert grabs his arm.)* Jack, don't leave like this.

JACK. I'm getting a drink.
ALBERT. I have some Jack Daniels in my room.
JACK. I'd rather be alone.
ALBERT. It's not a good thing to drink on one's own.
JACK. It is if you do it right.
ALBERT. Don't isolate, young man. Company is what you need. It just so happens I'm having a little poker party tonight and we're in need of a fourth hand.
JACK. I don't think so.
ALBERT. As I once told Elizabeth Taylor on the set of *Butterfield 8*, any port in a storm.
JACK. Albert, I don't want to be rude or anything, but I'm really not interested.
ALBERT. Too bad. It's a new bottle of that delectable Tennessee elixir.
JACK. Oh, what the hell.
ALBERT. Capital. Do you know our chauffeur?
JACK. Oh, shit. You mean Sonny?
ALBERT. He's a lousy card player but rather amusing to have around. How do you feel about priests? *(They cross to an area representing Albert's room where Sonny and Father Gabriel are seated at the table. As Jack and Albert join them, they all "toast" with shots of bourbon.)* Bottoms up. *(They clink glasses and down their shots, slamming the empty glasses to the table.)*
FATHER GABRIEL. This stuff's got more of a kick than altar wine. *(Sonny picks up the empty bottle.)*
SONNY. Another one bites the dust.
JACK. Albert, you got any more of this?
SONNY. You don't need any more. Half a dozen shots and you can't see straight.
ALBERT. My deal. *(Albert begins to deal the cards.)*
SONNY. I'm out of this hand. You're too good.
ALBERT. Suit yourself, Schlomo. May I tempt you with another card, Padre?
FATHER GABRIEL. Lead us not into temptation.
ALBERT. I was once supposed to play the serpent in a dance piece with Ann-Margaret. Pity, I'm allergic to apples.
FATHER GABRIEL. I hooked up with a girl named Margaret the night before I went into the seminary. *(All the guys lean in, interested.)*
SONNY. What did you do, Father G?
FATHER GABRIEL. Well, I met her at a bar and after a few

drinks, we decided to go skinny-dipping in the pond behind the old quarry.
SONNY. And then...?
FATHER GABRIEL. There we were ... naked ... in the water ... and we started kissing ... a lot.
SONNY. You dog, you.
FATHER GABRIEL. She wanted to go further and I really wanted to but I'd had way too many wine coolers. So, we made a date to meet back at the quarry the next night.
SONNY. Did you go? *(Father Gabriel shakes his head "no.")*
FATHER GABRIEL. I was so drunk I couldn't think straight. The next morning I woke up in the seminary with twenty-five men.
ALBERT. Sounds like a party at Elton John's.
SONNY. Man, you're never going to live this night down, Father G. I might have to come hear you preach some Sunday morning.
FATHER GABRIEL. Really?
SONNY. Hell, yeah. Drunk, chick, naked, moonlight. It'll be fun sitting in the first pew watching you squirm. *(Jack bangs his hand on the table.)*
JACK. Hit me again. *(Albert deals Jack another card.)* Twenty! Now, beat that! *(Jack starts to move the pile of dollar bills and coins towards himself.)*
ALBERT. Tut, tut! Not so fast, my boy. The queen of hearts is my up card and a gentleman must always respect Lady Luck. *(Albert flips over his down card.)* Eighteen. *(Albert takes a third card.)* Three of hearts. Twenty-one. *(Jack throws down his cards in despair.)*
JACK. Albert, that's the sixth hand in a row. Are you sure these cards aren't marked?
ALBERT. Perhaps this isn't your game. Let's try another. When I was just a boy, Eddie Robinson taught me how to do this on the set of *Little Caesar*. Or was it Caesar Romero on *The Adventures of Robin Hood*?
JACK. Caesar Romero wasn't in *The Adventures of Robin Hood*.
ALBERT. True. He'd never wear tights ... in public. Poor old Butch. *(Albert places three walnut shells on the table.)*
SONNY. You don't really expect him to fall for the old shell game, do you?
ALBERT. Even if it's his last chance to settle the score?
JACK. What the hell!
SONNY. Don't do it, man. You'll be sorry.
JACK. Double or nothing!

33

ALBERT. *Bravissimo!*
FATHER GABRIEL. This is so much more fun than bingo. *(Albert deftly maneuvers the shells around the table.)*
ALBERT. Now, keep your eye on the pea. This is an act of prestidigitation to rival anything concocted by Orson Welles. Now once more. And again. *Finis. (Albert looks at Sonny. Sonny nudges Jack and points to the middle shell.)*
SONNY. Middle one. Go for the middle one, man.
FATHER GABRIEL. No, no, no. I think it's the one on the right. *(Jack thinks for a moment.)*
JACK. You guys are wrong. It's under the left one. *(He points expectantly to the shell.)*
ALBERT. Tough break, old man!
SONNY. Told ya, man.
FATHER GABRIEL. I still can't believe you're Clara's son. She is a such a handful.
JACK. Don't I know it.
FATHER GABRIEL. I started praying very hard to Saint Jude when I began dealing with your mother. He's the patron saint of the Impossible!
JACK. How's that going?
FATHER GABRIEL. I'm still waiting.
SONNY. Well, guys, it's time to hit the road. Let's go, Father G, I'll drop you by the rectory on my way home.
FATHER GABRIEL. Oooh, could we stop for some ice cream?
SONNY. Sure, I've got the munchies too. *(Sonny and Father Gabriel exit.)*
JACK. I should probably get going myself. I hope Clara's asleep by now. *(Jack stands unsteadily.)* Albert. I think I'll go lie down.
ALBERT. But what about our game?
JACK. I declare you the champion.
ALBERT. Sophia Loren once said that to me after a dirty weekend in Reno … or was it Ursula Andres in Palm Springs? Be that as it may, I shall try my best, once again, to live up to the title. *(Jack stumbles out. Lights crossfade to Gertrude and Clara walking towards the hospital area.)*
GERTRUDE. I'm sorry you and Jack had words last night.
CLARA. After all these years, I think I prefer the silence.
GERTRUDE. Didn't he say anything to you when he came in last night?
CLARA. No, I didn't give him the chance. I pretended to be asleep

but I think he was drunk.
GERTRUDE. Not Jack.
CLARA. He was stumbling and thrashing around out in the living room for a while until he finally went to sleep.
GERTRUDE. Well, this will make you feel better. It's an absolutely amazing feeling. *(They put on sterile paper gowns. Gertrude adjusts the paper gown and gloves on Clara.)* Her name is Mai Ling. She's the most delicate little thing you've ever seen … so tiny and precious.
CLARA. Oh, I can hardly wait! *(Gertrude and Clara enter the baby holding area.)* Isn't anyone here?
GERTRUDE. It's always quiet at this time of day. *(Gertrude makes a beeline for the bassinet holding Mai Ling and gently takes the baby into her arms.)* Mai Ling, meet my best friend, Clara.
CLARA. How do you do, Mai Ling? You're even prettier than Gertrude said you'd be.
GERTRUDE. There's one for you. *(Clara cautiously picks up a baby.)*
CLARA. Hello, you sweet thing.
GERTRUDE. What's her name? *(Clara gently but awkwardly looks at the name tag on the baby's wrist. Her face drops.)*
CLARA. Kiki. Her name is Kiki. *(Beat.)* She's so beautiful. And they call her Kiki.
GERTRUDE. What is the world coming to when they give them names like that? That name belongs in a birdcage. When I think of the names of my girlhood chums, the Veronicas and the Charlottes …
CLARA. Isobel! *(The women stand very close together holding their cooing babies.)*
GERTRUDE. Isobel! And the Josephines. If Henry and I had a daughter, we'd have named her Josephine. *(Relishing the moment, Gertrude sings softly to Mai Ling.)* "Come, Josephine in my flying machine, in the air she goes, there she goes … " *(Gertrude splits her focus between singing to Mai Ling and singing to Clara. Clara smiles as she also remembers the song.)* "Balancing free like a bird on a beam in the air she goes … " *(Clara sings along, croaking with Gertrude note for note.)*
CLARA. "There she goes … " *(The women sing together as they rock their babies, laughing joyously.)*
GERTRUDE and CLARA. "Up, up a little bit higher, oh my, the moon is on fire. Come Josephine, in my flying machine going up, all on, goodbye." *(The women laugh with great abandon. Clara looks down at the happily gurgling Kiki. Gertrude beams down at Mai Ling*

but suddenly stops laughing. Frozen in place, her eyes fill with terror.)
GERTRUDE. Mai Ling? *(The baby is motionless in her arms.)* Mai Ling? *(Gertrude swallows hard and looks at Clara in panic.)* No … please … *(Overcome with emotion, Gertrude suddenly holds Mai Ling tightly to her breast. Gertrude moves, as if in slow motion, and sits in a chair. The tears in her eyes begin to stream down her cheeks. Clara puts down the baby in her arms and goes to Gertrude, stroking her hair and gently rubbing her shoulders.)*
CLARA. Shhhh … shhh … *(Gertrude holds the lifeless child as close as she can, rocking her slowly. She closes her eyes and drops her head back, sobbing — without emitting a sound. Lights up in the dining room, later the same day. Clara and Gertrude sit at the table with their trays in front of them.)* Please have a little something, dear … *(Gertrude doesn't reply.)* The beets look lovely today … *(Staring out into space, Gertrude remains silent.)* Maybe just a sip of tea? I know what happened to that little baby was tragic. But it was God's will.
GERTRUDE. She was such a beautiful little girl … oh, to be that young again and to have it all ahead of you. "Ring around the rosy, pocket full of posies, ashes, ashes, all fall down." They won't get up again for all the tea in China …
CLARA. Keep it up! You just keep on strolling down memory lane. They'll lock you up and you won't be able to manage your own affairs.
GERTRUDE. I don't have affairs.
CLARA. And when they ask me, I'll tell them you're not competent and can't be trusted.
GERTRUDE. And who can be?
CLARA. Me! You can trust me. *(Eyes narrowing, Gertrude leans to Clara, her voice even.)*
GERTRUDE. Oh, really? You used to repeat everything I told you in confidence to Henry. *(Clara looks aghast.)* I know you did, Clara. Henry told me so. *(Unseen by Gertrude, Clara momentarily grabs her side in pain.)*
CLARA. Then why did you keep telling me things?
GERTRUDE. Oh, I don't know. I guess I just wanted Henry to like you.
CLARA. You think Henry didn't like me? Did he say that?!
GERTRUDE. He said that in the beginning to throw me off the track. Later, he told me that he loved you. *(Shocked, Clara looks at Gertrude for a long moment.)*

CLARA. You knew?
GERTRUDE. Yes, dear.
CLARA. And you didn't leave him?
GERTRUDE. Of course not. I thought about it once, but I decided against it.
CLARA. But, why?
GERTRUDE. Because I didn't want to lose you.
CLARA. Doesn't it matter to you that your husband and your best friend were loving behind your back?
GERTRUDE. Love is so rare. Who am I to criticize where it's found? I'm happy to know that Henry discovered it before he died. And so close to home. Henry never did wander far from home. He loved my meatloaf ... my cookies ... my friends.
CLARA. Gertrude, have you no pride? On Henry's deathbed he asked me to look after you.
GERTRUDE. How sweet. *(Clara stares at Gertrude in amazement.)*
CLARA. That's the only thing I never wanted you to know. I was taking that secret to my grave. Gertrude, how could you?
GERTRUDE. Clara, I never meant to hurt you, dear! When I was thinking of leaving Henry, I was so miserable. I knew if I left him, I'd lose you, too. And you think twice about losing a friend after forty.
CLARA. All these years you've known. You've placed your faith in me and I've been so untruthful.
GERTRUDE. No, you haven't ...
CLARA. Of course, I have! I have a whole box of love letters from him!
GERTRUDE. He wrote to you? Isn't that nice!
CLARA. Henry and I loved each other right up to his death.
GERTRUDE. Yes, and you'll love me right up to mine.
CLARA. And to think I thought I knew every hair on your head. *(Beat.)*
GERTRUDE. Clara, how did you and Henry know you had true love?
CLARA. I don't think we knew it as much as we deduced it. You understand? *(Gertrude shakes her head "no.")* Well, we knew we hadn't found it elsewhere, so we figured we had it. If the pea isn't under the other walnut shell, you deduce it's under yours. *(Gertrude gently turns and speaks very deliberately.)*
GERTRUDE. That's what I wanted to know. Did Henry look under your walnut shell?
CLARA. No.

GERTRUDE. Why not?
CLARA. We were afraid.
GERTRUDE. Afraid of me?
CLARA. No, afraid the pea might not be there.
GERTRUDE. That was the only part I wasn't sure of. Now, we won't speak of it anymore.
CLARA. If only there was some way I could make it up to you.
GERTRUDE. It's not necessary, dear. *(Gertrude's eyes become very wide.)* But … there is something … *(Clara studies Gertrude's face intently.)*
CLARA. What is it?
GERTRUDE. Do you really want me to tell you?
CLARA. Yes!
GERTRUDE. Take me with you.
CLARA. Where?
GERTRUDE. To your mausoleum.
CLARA. But, it isn't even built yet.
GERTRUDE. I know, but I want to go there with you. We can plan it together. Then I'll know that when the time comes, there'll be room for me, too!
CLARA. You mean you want to be buried with me?!
GERTRUDE. Yes, oh yes! May I … please?
CLARA. I suppose so. I suppose it could be arranged.
GERTRUDE. You're making me so happy, Clara! I've always hated being alone. *(The women look deeply into each other's eyes for a moment. As Gertrude starts to embrace her, Clara breaks the spell abruptly.)*
CLARA. Then, it's all settled. I have a lot of catalogues to show you. We might like something other than a mausoleum. They have vaults, and serenity spots.
GERTRUDE. Oh, they all sound lovely.
CLARA. Well, we'd better get a move on. We have a busy day ahead of us. *(Clara rises and once again grabs her side in pain.)*
GERTRUDE. Clara, would you wait for me? I'll just be a moment.
CLARA. All right, dear. I'll wait right here. *(Clara sits back down again, holding her side. Gertrude starts to exit and then returns and places her hands lovingly on Clara's shoulders from behind.)*
GERTRUDE. Oh, Clara, it means so much to have a friend waiting. *(Gertrude exits. Lights crossfade to Clara's apartment, Jack snores on the loveseat. Sonny enters with a paper cup. He stands over Jack. Sonny clamps Jack's nose shut. After a moment Jack wakes with a start*

then grabs his head in pain.)
SONNY. Wake up, sunshine. Day's half over.
JACK. Can't you ever just knock? *(Sonny pounds on the table once. Jack grabs Sonny's arm to stop him. Sonny offers the cup.)*
SONNY. Brought you a prairie oyster.
JACK. I can't even think of food. I'm barely breathing.
SONNY. This is the best thing for a hangover.
JACK. Really?
SONNY. Yeah. A raw egg, some Worcester sauce and a few of my own special ingredients and you'll be just fine. *(Jack takes the cup and begins to drink the contents, grimacing.)* Or throw your guts up. *(Jack races to the bathroom and vomits. He reenters, wiping his mouth. Sonny crosses to the table and sits.)* Feel better?
JACK. I will once I'm on that plane.
SONNY. You going somewhere?
JACK. Back to Seattle.
SONNY. What about Clara?
JACK. She's doing just fine without me.
SONNY. Wrong, man. Besides, you've got plenty of unfinished business.
JACK. I don't give a damn what you think. What're you doing here anyway?
SONNY. Wednesday. One o'clock. Dr. Sanders.
JACK. Why is she going to the doctor again?
SONNY. She's old, Einstein.
JACK. Clara hates doctors, always has. What's going on?
SONNY. Thought you didn't give a damn.
JACK. Don't be a smart-ass. Tell me.
SONNY. Not my place, man. My job is getting stoned and driving old folks around. Her job is being a pain in the ass and telling everybody to go to hell.
JACK. She ought to have a gold watch by now.
SONNY. But that's who she is. You can't keep running away. You've got to stay and fix this.
JACK. So that's my job.
SONNY. If you ask me, you and your mom both screwed up.
JACK. Look, I know you mean well, but I really don't think this concerns you.
SONNY. Wrong again, man. It does. I care about the old broad and I think you do, too. Stop laying a guilt trip on her. It's time for you to be the grown-up. *(Clara enters.)*

JACK. Where've you been?
CLARA. Out. Some people don't sleep all day. Sonny, we can go now.
SONNY. Toots, I just came by to tell you that I couldn't drive you today.
CLARA. But you always drive me.
SONNY. Yeah, but since you've got Aloysius here, I figured I could work in some new clients and earn some extra scratch for the time being. *(Sonny grabs Jack's rental car keys from the table and tosses them to him.)* Can you handle that, sunshine?
JACK. Sure.
CLARA. Well, go and brush your teeth. You can drop me off and pick me up later after you'd had the time to make yourself more presentable. *(To Sonny.)* And I'm officially mad at you.
SONNY. Sorry, Clara, but you're in good hands. Just tell him where to go.
JACK. She's good at that. *(Lights transition to Jack and Clara in the "car." After a while, Clara speaks, keeping her eyes front.)*
CLARA. You didn't have to take me, you know. I could have called a cab. Then you could have stayed home on the phone with your minions.
JACK. I'm sorry about that but I still have to work.
CLARA. Such a busy little man.
JACK. I'd like to try and understand about you and Dad and Uncle Henry. Can we talk about it?
CLARA. Talking won't change the past.
JACK. No, but it might make it easier for me to deal with.
CLARA. I don't see how. *(Pause.)*
JACK. Is a mausoleum that important to you?
CLARA. Yes, it is. Since I can't be buried next to the man I loved and won't be buried next to the man who stopped loving me, I have to be on my own. *(The two ride for a while longer in silence. Jack motions out the window.)*
JACK. You know how many people are buried in Forest Lawn? *(Clara shakes her head "no.")* All of 'em. *(Clara smiles despite herself.)*
CLARA. That was one of your father's lame jokes.
JACK. Remember the first time he told us that joke? The car trip to Santa Fe? I was twelve.
CLARA. Ugh, I got so carsick. But you had to see some real Indians.
JACK. I saved my allowance for a month so I could buy you some

genuine turquoise earrings for Mother's Day. *(Turning away from him, Clara looks at the scenery passing by the window.)*
CLARA. Ugly, big clunky things.
JACK. I thought they were beautiful!
CLARA. When you sneaked away to that trading post to buy them, I thought you were lost. I was so scared that when you came back, I whacked you in the head.
JACK. No, you slapped me across the face. *(Beat.)* Then I handed you the earrings.
CLARA. How was I to know? I was frantic. *(Fighting to keep her emotions in check, Clara points ahead.)* Turn left at the light. Your father should have told me where you'd gone.
JACK. It was supposed to be a surprise.
CLARA. It was.
JACK. Didn't you love him … even a little?
CLARA. Maybe once … a little. He was so crazy about you that he wanted to spend all his time with you.
JACK. I thought everybody's dad was like that.
CLARA. He didn't have room in his life for both of us. You were a child, you had to win. So I turned to Henry.
JACK. Didn't the thought of Aunt Gertrude bother you?
CLARA. All the time! That's why it never went further than … it went.
JACK. And how far was that?
CLARA. It's the third building on the right. *(Unseen by Jack, Clara holds her side and winces in pain as she gets out of the car.)*
JACK. Do you want me to go in with you?
CLARA. No. Thanks. Come back in an hour.
JACK. Maybe I can take you for a bite to eat later?
CLARA. That'd be nice. As long as I don't have to eat quiche. *(Jack shakes his head and laughs to himself as he exits. Lights crossfade to the dining room. Father Gabriel enters, sees Gertrude sitting at the table and tries to exit. She spots him.)*
GERTRUDE. Father Gabriel. Can I speak with you for a moment?
FATHER GABRIEL. This isn't a good time. *(He tries to rush out.)*
GERTRUDE. Slow down, please. *(Father Gabriel stops.)*
FATHER GABRIEL. What is it?
GERTRUDE. Will there be some kind of a service for Mai Ling?
FATHER GABRIEL. No.
GERTRUDE. That's odd. I thought for sure you'd do something.

FATHER GABRIEL. There will be a funeral but you can't attend.
GERTRUDE. Why not?
FATHER GABRIEL. It's just for the family.
GERTRUDE. I loved that little baby just like she was my own.
FATHER GABRIEL. Mrs. Wynant ...
GERTRUDE. Gertrude.
FATHER GABRIEL. MRS. WYNANT! Why did you go in there when I told you not to?
GERTRUDE. I was bored doing the things you had for me, and I didn't think ...
FATHER GABRIEL. That's right, you didn't think, and look what happened.
GERTRUDE. I didn't mean any harm.
FATHER GABRIEL. You weren't properly trained! *(Gertrude stops abruptly.)*
GERTRUDE. Father Gabriel, I know how to hold a baby.
FATHER GABRIEL. Mrs. Wynant, the baby died!
GERTRUDE. You think I don't know that? Stop treating me like an incompetent old fool. I haven't been able to think of anything else.
FATHER GABRIEL. I can understand that.
GERTRUDE. But it wasn't my fault.
FATHER GABRIEL. Your boredom put my job, the program and the entire hospital in jeopardy. Haven't you done enough?
GERTRUDE. I was only trying to help.
FATHER GABRIEL. This doesn't seem to be working. Mrs. Wynant, I think it best that you don't return to the volunteer program.
GERTRUDE. My love isn't what killed her ... it's what kept her alive.
FATHER GABRIEL. I'm through with this discussion. Mrs. Wynant, you cannot attend the funeral.
GERTRUDE. Just who do you think you are, anyway?
FATHER GABRIEL. Excuse me?
GERTRUDE. You think you know what people need, but do you ever ask them? All you know is what you want. If you weren't trying so hard to impress everyone with how good you think you are, maybe you really would be.
FATHER GABRIEL. This is not about me.
GERTRUDE. I think it is. You're not a priest, not really. You don't have the faintest idea about how to help someone. All you do is play with balloons and run around making up committees. I

thought priests were supposed to comfort people at a time of grief, not make them feel worse. I may be afraid of death, but you, Gabe, are afraid of life. *(Beat.)* Maybe you shouldn't go back to the program until you know what it's really about.

FATHER GABRIEL. The service is at 4:00 today. *(Gertrude exits, leaving Father Gabriel alone. Lights crossfade to Clara and Sonny in the car downstage. He drives while she looks out the window. Sonny steers with one hand while adeptly rolling a joint. He speaks over his shoulder to Clara in the back seat.)*

SONNY. I do not believe you skipped out on Mr. Fortune 500. He's going to be one pissed-off dude when he gets back to the doctor's office. That's not really going to help, Clara. *(Sonny licks the joint to seal it.)*

CLARA. I just can't face him right now.

SONNY. You're gonna have to tell him sooner or later.

CLARA. I get so uptight when I'm around him. I always have.

SONNY. Maybe a little of this would help. Maui Wowie. Excellent bud. *(He holds up the joint to Clara, who looks at it in disgust.)* Hey, don't knock it till you've tried it. Queen Victoria smoked it for menstrual cramps.

CLARA. No kidding? *(Sonny takes another toke and holds the joint out to Clara. She looks at it for a long moment before the lights fade. In the darkness, Clara and Sonny cross to the dining area and sit at the table. As the lights come up, Clara's plate is loaded with food. Sonny and Clara laugh hysterically.)* God, I'm starving!

SONNY. Go easy, toots, don't want to make yourself sick. *(Surveying her laden tray, Clara grabs a bowl and a spoon.)*

CLARA. Mmmm! This is the best bread pudding I've ever eaten. It's smooth as silk. *(Sonny laughs as Albert enters.)*

SONNY. Speak of the devil! Here's ol' smooth moves himself … *(Spotting Clara, Albert quickly crosses to her with a flourish.)*

ALBERT. Be still my heart!

CLARA. If that's the way you want it! *(Clara rises, grabs Albert by his lapels, dips him and plants a big kiss on him. Albert, looking terrified, gasps for breath and wanders away in a stupor.)* That'll fix 'im. *(She gives Sonny a "high five" and sits back down to her feast. They both laugh uncontrollably. Unseen by Clara, Jack enters.)*

JACK. How could you do that to me?

CLARA. What? *(Clara turns and faces Jack. She stops laughing abruptly.)*

JACK. You think it's funny to ask me to come pick you up and

just disappear? I thought you'd wandered off, been in an accident, or worse. Then I find you here, wasted.
CLARA. Keep your voice down!
JACK. Go into the ladies room and put some cold water on your face. We're leaving. Now! *(Clara debates for a moment, then without looking at either of them, exits to the ladies' room.)* How could you be so stupid?!
SONNY. Jack, man, she's scared.
JACK. Bullshit! She's never been scared of anything in her life!
SONNY. Maybe not before, but now …
JACK. But "now" what?
SONNY. She's dying. She's got a month or two … three, tops. *(Jack stares at Sonny, totally stunned.)* She didn't know how to tell you.
JACK. When did she…?
SONNY. About forty-five minutes ago. *(Clara reenters from the ladies' room, still not looking at either one of them. Sonny turns to her.)* Clara, I told him.
JACK. I'm sorry, I … *(She looks deep into Jack's eyes.)*
CLARA. Don't tell Gertrude.
JACK. But …
CLARA. Promise me.
JACK. I don't …
CLARA. PROMISE ME!
JACK. I promise.
CLARA. Let's go. *(Dappled lighting and a stone bench suggest a military cemetery. Jack enters and walks to a shady, out-of-the-way spot. He stares down at a grave marker.)*
JACK. Hey, Pop … surprise. You're a hard man to find. *(His eyes uncontrollably fill with tears.)* Did you know? Do you know now? So much is going on. My head's all screwed up. Clara's telling me all this stuff and I don't know what to believe. Is it true? *(Beat.)* Pop, I don't know what to do about anything. *(Father Gabriel enters, holding a balloon.)*
FATHER GABRIEL. Jack. What are you doing here?
JACK. I needed to talk to my dad.
FATHER GABRIEL. You didn't have to come here for that.
JACK. Uh, what's with the balloon?
FATHER GABRIEL. It's for Mai Ling. I use it to symbolize the soul's journey upwa … *(He looks at the balloon for a long moment.)* It's nothing, actually. Just an old habit. *(He releases the balloon.)* As long as I'm here, do you think you might want to talk to me?

JACK. You?
FATHER GABRIEL. Well, you don't really know me so it would be an anonymous confession.
JACK. Father, I haven't been in a church or said a prayer in years.
FATHER GABRIEL. That doesn't matter, really. Hey, I told you about Margaret and me at the quarry that night. Just think of it as two guys talking.
JACK. I left town ... ran away nearly twenty years ago.
FATHER GABRIEL. Why?
JACK. *(Hesitates.)* Wanted to vanish into thin air. *(Beat.)* I kept in touch with my pop and he knew where I was. After a while, I guess he felt he had to tell Clara. When I wouldn't talk to her, she wrote me a letter but I threw it in a drawer unopened. I thought that would be the end of it. But they kept coming. Look, I don't know what she's told you, but ...
FATHER GABRIEL. Jack, it would be a sacrilege to reveal anything Clara told me.
JACK. Just before I graduated I cut class one day to come home and just chill out before finals. I saw my mother ... with her best friend's husband.
FATHER GABRIEL. *(Stunned.)* With ... Gertrude's husband?
JACK. Yes.
FATHER GABRIEL. Were they being intimate?
JACK. No, but they looked so flustered and guilty when they saw me. It wasn't difficult to figure out what was going on.
FATHER GABRIEL. And so you left.
JACK. The sight of Clara and Uncle Henry sent me into a rage. I mean, how could she do that to my dad? I didn't know what else to do, so I ran away. I stayed with friends until I got out of school and then I split.
FATHER GABRIEL. The path of least resistance.
JACK. I know it was stupid, but it was all I could think of. I lied to him about why I left until the day he died. I mean, he knew something was wrong, but only asked me about it once. He said I could tell him when I was ready, but I never did.
FATHER GABRIEL. Don't you suppose he knew?
JACK. Maybe. I don't know. We were very easy together. But, when Clara was around, it felt like I was competing with her for his love. And now ...
FATHER GABRIEL. What's changed?
JACK. I learned that my Dad's human after all. He chose me over

Clara and that drove her to Uncle Henry. Nice, huh? I've been in the middle of a tug of war since I was born.

FATHER GABRIEL. Jack, don't you think the contest is over? You have to forgive your dad, Clara and Gertrude's husband.

JACK. Why are you defending them?

FATHER GABRIEL. It's in my job description. Besides, it must have been difficult for them.

JACK. That's not the kind of thing I expected you to say.

FATHER GABRIEL. I know. I'm kind of surprised myself. Jack, everybody makes mistakes but what's important is how we deal with them. Some people punch the wall, others get drunk. Let Clara off the hook. You're only punishing yourself. *(Beat.)* Since this was supposed to be a confession, for your penance say four "Our Fathers" and three "Hail Marys." *(Father Gabriel crosses himself.)*

JACK. If I can remember how.

FATHER GABRIEL. Do your best. *(Father Gabriel starts to exit and meets Gertrude as she enters.)* Gertrude, I'm glad you're here. We'll be up on the hill, under under the pine tree.

GERTRUDE. Thank you. I'll be there in a minute. *(She crosses to Jack.)* This is the only part of the cemetery that doesn't frighten me. Maybe because it isn't sacred ground. The military doesn't have the graves blessed like the church does. Did you know that, Jack? *(Jack shakes his head "no.")* But that's what Henry wanted. I come to visit him and keep him up to date about what's going on in the world. He was always so preoccupied in life that much of it passed him by. *(Gertrude takes a hankie from her coat pocket and wipes a tear from Jack's eye.)* Your mother is very glad you're here. She did miss you, you know.

JACK. I know. I did what I thought I had to do.

GERTRUDE. We all did, dear, and it's all right. Everything's fine. Now, I must go to say goodbye to Mai Ling. *(Lights fade as they exit. Clara enters downstage left to the church area, which now represents a confessional. Father Gabriel leans against a screen finishing a prayer.)*

FATHER GABRIEL. … and I absolve you of your sins in the name of the Father, and of the Son and of the Holy Spirit. Amen. *(Father Gabriel pauses as the next confessor enters in the shadows.)* Welcome, my child. How have you…? *(Before he can finish, Clara's voice stops him.)*

CLARA. I'm not here to confess, Gabe.

FATHER GABRIEL. Clara, this is not the time. I don't know if I

have the strength for you right now.
CLARA. That's too bad. I need guidance.
FATHER GABRIEL. And you came to me?
CLARA. You're all I've got.
FATHER GABRIEL. I just don't know what to say to you that could help.
CLARA. I'll make it easy for you. I need to know when it's okay to go. *(Father Gabriel hesitates.)*
FATHER GABRIEL. What?
CLARA. You heard me.
FATHER GABRIEL. "Go" as in … die?
CLARA. Yes.
FATHER GABRIEL. Clara, God decides when it's time. You know that.
CLARA. What if Gertrude's right? What if He forgets?
FATHER GABRIEL. He has a plan and we cannot question it.
CLARA. You sound like you're reading out of a prayer book. I knew this was a mistake. *(She gets up to leave.)*
FATHER GABRIEL. No! Wait! Wait! You're right. *(Beat.)* Sit down, Clara, let's figure this out. *(Beat.)* Why are you asking this? *(On the verge of tears, Clara fights to hold them back.)*
CLARA. Because I hurt too much to go on. Every day is a challenge. Sometimes it's all I can do to get out of bed and make it to the sink before I vomit.
FATHER GABRIEL. I see.
CLARA. No, you don't see! Gabe, I don't believe that's part of His plan. I don't want to live like this.
FATHER GABRIEL. Are you asking for permission to take your life? *(A long silence. Father Gabriel speaks softly to her in a comforting tone.)* If you do, you will never be admitted to the Kingdom of Heaven.
CLARA. Do you really believe that?
FATHER GABRIEL. It's not important if I believe it.
CLARA. Don't play games with me.
FATHER GABRIEL. I'm not. Clara, you have to trust in God.
CLARA. My God or your God? My God is all-forgiving!
FATHER GABRIEL. So is mine, Clara, He loves all of us in spite of who we are and what we've done, but … we're His children and He'd no sooner hurt us … than you would hurt Jack.
CLARA. But I did.
FATHER GABRIEL. So, you're not perfect. You made a few mis-

takes.

CLARA. More than a few, Gabe.

FATHER GABRIEL. So what?

CLARA. That's it? Those are your words of wisdom?

FATHER GABRIEL. I don't have any words of wisdom. Believe me, I know it's hard to have faith sometimes. But God understands what we do. Take comfort in that. He knows what's in your heart. You have to forgive yourself, Clara. He already has. *(A long silence.)*

CLARA. Thank you … Father Gabriel. *(Clara exits. Father Gabriel is silent, partly because of Clara's declaration … and partly because it's the first time she's ever called him "Father.")*

FATHER GABRIEL. Clara, I … Clara? *(Silence. Father Gabriel exits the confessional and looks for Clara but the church is empty.)* God be with you, Mrs. Olsen. *(Father Gabriel exits as Gertrude enters from the opposite side of the stage. She sits on the bench.)*

GERTRUDE. Hello … God? Can I talk to you? Oh. *(She incorrectly makes the sign of the cross.)* I don't know the kind of prayers Clara says, but I know she feels better after she does. I need to ask you for a favor. Do people do that? Just come out and say, "Can you help me, here?" Well, it's like this. Clara thinks she can do it alone, but she can't … and I don't think you want her to, if you don't mind my saying. I mean, you had us both there for Mai Ling. And I still don't know why you did that. Just when we were all so happy. Forgive me for saying so, but that wasn't nice. Father Gabriel said Mai Ling needed to know someone loved her and I did give her that. If she died knowing she was loved, maybe it wasn't so bad for her. Is that what Clara needs, too? Well, if that's what you want for her, I'm not sure I'm enough. But if you'll give me a just a little bit of help … thanks for listening. Oh, um … Amen. *(Gertrude makes the sign of the cross correctly this time. She exits. Crossfade to Clara's apartment. Albert enthusiastically knocks on the door.)*

ALBERT. *(Offstage.)* Clara? Clara? *(Clara enters from the bedroom and shaking her head, goes to the door.)*

CLARA. I'm busy, Albert. Go away. *(He knocks again.)*

ALBERT. *(Offstage.)* I have wonderful news. *(Clara gives in and opens the door.)*

CLARA. Make it fast. *(Albert proudly struts into the room.)*

ALBERT. After a considerable amount of campaigning and oozing enviable charm, I managed to wear down the selection committee. You are looking at the new occupant of room 329, the apartment with

the breathtaking southern exposure vacated by poor old whoosiz.
CLARA. His name was Edgar.
ALBERT. Why, so it was. Poor old Edgar.
CLARA. Gertrude remembered. She remembers a lot.
ALBERT. I wonder if dear Gertrude will make me some new curtains?
CLARA. Ask her yourself on your way out. Goodbye, Albert.
ALBERT. How are you, my dear?
CLARA. Not so great at the moment.
ALBERT. So then, you *are* sick.
CLARA. What's the point in talking about it?
ALBERT. Clara, you know how much I care for you. And that kiss told me that you are not indifferent to me.
CLARA. That was the Maui Wowie.
ALBERT. Whatever the reason, we have many years behind us and I often think of what might have been. When I'm settled in my new digs, I will be able to entertain once again. It'll be just like the parties at Errol Flynn's. We used to throw tipsy starlets into the pool. One time, Errol and I dangled a …
CLARA. Albert, that's enough! Stop making things up! You never threw tipsy starlets into a pool, you didn't know any of those people and you were never more than an extra!
ALBERT. *(Quietly.)* I was always more than an extra … but no one ever saw it. We all have to have our dreams, Clara. You have no right to shatter mine.
CLARA. You're right, Albert. I'm sorry.
ALBERT. Thank you. I would consider it an honor if you'd be my first guest. Won't you come to tea?
CLARA. That might be nice.
ALBERT. I shall look forward to it.
CLARA. Good night, sweet prince. *(Albert takes her hand and kisses it. She gently touches his cheek. Sonny enters.)*
SONNY. Get a room, you two.
CLARA. He was just leaving.
SONNY. Hey man, congrats on the new pad.
ALBERT. My own little den of iniquity. The chicks will love it. *(Albert exits. Clara crosses to the sofa. Sonny closes the door.)*
CLARA. He'll never change. So … where is it?
SONNY. You sure about this?
CLARA. Have you ever known me to be wishy-washy? *(Sonny reaches into his pocket and pulls out a plastic bag of colorful pills.)*

SONNY. How many?
CLARA. As many as it takes to kill the pain.
SONNY. Did you ask your doctor for anything?
CLARA. His aren't strong enough. *(Sonny opens the bag and counts out ten pale yellow pills. Clara lines them up on the table.)*
SONNY. These are good for pain.
CLARA. What are they?
SONNY. It's called OxyContin. On the street it's known as "Hillbilly Heroin." Now, they're really strong and illegal as hell. If anybody finds out where you got these …
CLARA. Oh, get over it! How many?
SONNY. One a day. But only if the pain is really bad. Never more than that. And don't break it.
CLARA. Why not?
SONNY. It's a time-released narcotic. If you break the seal, the whole thing goes into your bloodstream all at once.
CLARA. Thank you, "Dr. Feelgood."
SONNY. Clara, I'm serious. It would be really easy to O.D. on these babies. I want to be sure that you know what you're doing. *(Clara holds her side and winces in pain.)*
CLARA. It's time for my nap. I'm getting cranky.
SONNY. You're telling me? *(Sonny kisses her on the cheek and exits. Lights fade to suggest a passage of time. After a moment, Jack stands nearby while Clara talks on his cell phone.)*
CLARA. … Ooo, you sound like such a big boy … yes, I will … here's your daddy.
JACK. Yeah, Charlie, she is pretty cool … uh-huh … I'm on my way to the airport now … okay, one souvenir … I'll see you sometime Monday. Right. Bye. *(Jack hangs up the phone.)*
CLARA. He sounds like a good boy.
JACK. He is. *(Beat.)* You sure you don't want me to stay until …
CLARA. Until I die?
JACK. I didn't want to say it.
CLARA. It's easier to say it than to do it.
JACK. How are you feeling?
CLARA. About the same. At least the shooting pains have stopped.
JACK. Any point in seeing the doc … *(Before he can finish, Clara simply raises her hand as if to say, "Don't bother.")*
CLARA. I'm cold.
JACK. I'll get your sweater. *(Jack looks at the monogram as he hands*

Clara the sweater.) He must have really been something.
CLARA. Who?
JACK. Uncle Henry. To have stayed with Aunt Gertrude all those years when he was in love with you.
CLARA. Those were different times. In my day, people learned to love one another as best they could.
JACK. Sort of like you and me?
CLARA. Maybe.
JACK. I've been thinking about the mausoleum.
CLARA. Really? So have I.
JACK. It'll be tight for a while, but I think you should have it.
CLARA. Thanks, but I don't want it.
JACK. What?!
CLARA. I want a serenity spot.
JACK. What's that?
CLARA. A serenity spot? It's a little area with lovely plantings and a bench with my name engraved on a marble wall. *(Jack smiles at her thoughtfully.)*
JACK. It sounds very peaceful.
CLARA. It will be a pretty place for you and little Charlie to visit.
JACK. And a helluva lot cheaper than a mausoleum. *(They laugh again.)*
CLARA. You're a lot like me sometimes.
JACK. Yeah, I guess I am. *(Jack begins to sway, taking Clara with him. He starts to sing "Little Brown Jug" and gently jitterbugs with Clara.)* "Ha, ha, ha, you and me … "
CLARA. "Little brown jug, don't I love thee?" *(They continue for a moment or two, then Clara stops.)* I love you, Jack. *(Stopped by her words, Jack, turns back to her.)*
JACK. I know, Mama. I love you, too. *(Jack crosses quickly to Clara and embraces her awkwardly. They hold the hug for a long moment.)*
CLARA. That's enough. It's time for me to go. *(Lights transition to show a passage of time. A worn recording of "Blue Moon" plays softly in the empty apartment. Freshly bathed and wearing a faded silk robe, Clara enters holding two small ivory envelopes. She crosses to the table and places the envelopes side by side. She crosses to the chair and takes the sweater. Folding it, she places it on the table with one of the letters resting on top. She crosses to the table and breaks the OxyContin tablets. She goes to her jewelry case and takes out the clunky turquoise earrings Jack bought her in Santa Fe. Holding them to the light, Clara studies them carefully and puts them on. She looks at her reflection.*

Unseen by Clara, Gertrude stands in the doorway.)
GERTRUDE. *(Offstage.)* I've always loved those earrings. *(Startled, Clara turns to see Gertrude standing in the doorway.)*
CLARA. This isn't a good time. I've got things to do.
GERTRUDE. I know. Sonny told me. He can never resist my chocolate chip cookies.
CLARA. Did you bring one for me? *(Gertrude takes out a cookie in a napkin from her purse and places it on the counter.)*
GERTRUDE. Let me make you some tea.
CLARA. No. Just sit with me. *(Gertrude glances at the coffee table and sees a neatly arranged line of the pale yellow pills and a tumbler of water.)*
GERTRUDE. Is there anything I can do?
CLARA. I don't think so.
GERTRUDE. Do you want me to go with you? *(Looking deeply into her friend's eyes, Clara clasps Gertrude's hands.)*
CLARA. No ... but, thank you.
GERTRUDE. I would, you know.
CLARA. I know. *(They sit in silence for a long moment. Suddenly, Clara clutches her side in great pain. It leaves almost as quickly as it came.)* Oh, by the way, I told Jack we're not going to have a mausoleum. He likes the idea of a serenity spot.
GERTRUDE. I'm glad. *(A second pain leaves Clara breathless. Gertrude hands the water glass and several broken pills to Clara.)* Be sure to introduce Henry to Mai Ling.
CLARA. Oh, what a lovely idea.
GERTRUDE. I'm sure they'll be great friends.
CLARA. Would you hand me my cookie? *(Gertrude notices the sweater and the two letters on the table.)*
GERTRUDE. You sure about the tea?
CLARA. Just the cookie. *(Gertrude gently strokes the sweater and then puts it on. She walks back to the couch.)* It looks better on you. *(She sits next to Clara, handing her the cookie. Taking a bite, Clara places her head in Gertrude's lap. Gently stroking Clara's hair, Gertrude begins to rock her and sing softly.)*
GERTRUDE. "Come Josephine in my flying machine, in the air she goes, there she goes, balancing free like a bird on a beam in the air she goes, there she goes ... " *(Breathlessly joining in, Clara tries to sing with Gertrude.)*
GERTRUDE and CLARA. "Up, up a little bit higher, oh my, the moon is on fire. Come Josephine in my flying machine ... " *(Clara's voice drops out and Gertrude finishes the song.)*

GERTRUDE. "Going up, all on … " *(Spoken.)* Goodbye. *(Gertrude continues to stroke Clara's hair. Lights fade. Curtain.)*

End of Play

PROPERTY LIST

Coffin, open, with corpse
Purse
Tape measure
Gloves
Hat
White balloon on string
2 cafeteria trays with sliced turkey, mashed potatoes, green beans, gravy
Silverware rolled in napkins, dessert, tea
Envelope, ripped in half each show
Briefcase
Overnight bag
Cell phone
Blackberry pager
Antique pocket watch
Custard, spoon
Roll in white paper napkin
Joint, *Metamorphoses*, iPod with headphones
Coat, monogrammed cardigan sweater (preset on sofa)
Bag of groceries, ring
From closet: shoebox with bills, etc., blue ribbon award, second shoebox with white wedding shoes and letters
Tea cups with lemon slices
Cafeteria tray with "lunch," orange (preset in dining room)
Desk, office chair, visitor chair with stacks of files
Father Gabriel — clipboard with paper, pen
3 Bassinets (two with "infants")
Rocking chair
Paper gown, latex gloves
"Dinner" set at kitchen counter
Burnt rolls in oven
In fridge: Waldorf salad, quiche, chocolate cake
Neat stack of bills, pen, envelope, shoebox
Cards, coins, dollar bills (preset in dining room)
Jack Daniels (almost empty bottle), 4 shot glasses
3 walnut shells, "pea"
Paper cup with hangover cure
Jack's rental car keys (preset in room)
Cigarette papers, matches/lighter

Bag with multiple Rx bottles, 10 yellow pills
Silk robe
Turquoise earrings in jewelry box (on dresser)
Pills, glass of water (preset)
Chocolate chip cookie

NOTE: Consumable props, such as food in the dining room, are not necessary and may be suggested stylistically.

SOUND EFFECTS

Lunch room conversation
Phone rings